Crime

Margaret McAlister

HORWITZ
MARTIN

HORWITZ MARTIN

Horwitz Martin Education
A Division of Horwitz
Publications Pty Ltd
55 Chandos St
St Leonards NSW 2065
Australia

Horwitz Martin Education
Unit 15, Cressex Enterprise Centre
Lincoln Road
High Wycombe, Bucks HP12 3RL
United Kingdom

First published 1999

a black dog book
Designed by Josie Semmler
Illustrations by Peter Mather pp. 3, 7, 13, 15, 18, 26, 27, 31, 32, 45, 48, 59, 62, 67, 72. Cover illustration by Mini Goss.
The editor would like to thank the following for permission to reproduce images: Queensland Police, p. 9; South Australian Police, pp. 10, 17, 21, 24, 28, 90, 91; Victoria Forensic Science Centre–Victoria Police, pp. 44, 53; Victoria Police, p. 49.
Other images are from the editor's, author's and designer's collections or are in the public domain. Every effort has been made to contact original sources, where known, for permissions. If an infringement has inadvertently occurred, the editor wishes to apologise. The editor and the publisher would like to thank Garry Chapman and Vicki Hazell,
the educational consultants for the series.

National Library of Australia
Cataloguing information
McAlister, Margaret.
Crime Night.

ISBN 0 7253 1661 6.

I. Title. (Series: Phenomena).

A823.3

Printed and bound in Australia
by Sands Print Group Ltd
2 3 4 5
00 01 02

Understanding the Horwitz Martin logo

Thoth
The Egyptian
god of wisdom,
mathematics and writing.

Contents

chapter 1
Night surveillance

IN THE SEMI-DARKNESS of his room, Ric glanced at the bright figures on the clock radio. Just after nine. All the kitchen noises had ceased, so it probably wouldn't be long now before his sister Gabby made her move.

He could just imagine how his parents would freak if they knew that Gabby sneaked out two or three times a week to meet that gang who hung around the video shop. Ric knew exactly how often she went out. He'd started keeping a surveillance log of her movements weeks ago, just like real detectives. It might be years yet before he could go into the police force, but he was determined to practise every chance he got.

surveillance log: *watching and recording someone's movements.*

Specialist police teams are trained in surveillance procedures, which may involve taking photographs, using a video camera, using microphones and taking notes.

Ric had read lots about being on surveillance. It was mostly dead boring, the books said. Hours and hours of waiting and observing and making notes about who came and went and what cars arrived and all that sort of thing. Sometimes the cops used cameras, sometimes videos and microphones—sometimes they didn't. Nowadays, if necessary, they brought in a specialist surveillance team that was trained to do nothing else. They kept logs. Just like he was doing.

His thoughts were interrupted by a faint noise from the room next door. Ric silently swung his feet to the floor and moved to his partly open window. He knew Gabby couldn't see him through the venetians at night; not without a light on behind him. He peered out. It was brighter outside than it was in his room: almost a full moon.

Gabby's window was only a metre or so from his. Her bag hit the window with a soft thunk as she clambered out. In the still night air, Ric heard her swear under her breath. Then she flitted past his window, her profile briefly lit by the moon, her nose-ring glinting. She never wore it in front of her parents. He watched while she slipped through the side gate, and waited for the sound that always followed her night excursions—the low rumble of a car starting up. Sure enough, he heard the engine turn over, and the car roared away with a screech of tyres.

Ric knew the car. One night when he'd been fairly certain Gabby was going to sneak out, he'd hopped out of his own window first and hidden behind a hedge a couple of houses up the road. He had watched while a black Holden rolled to a stop and waited for fifteen minutes. A window rolled down, and he could hear the low laughter of Briggsey and his friends coming from the car.

His mother would have been real happy about Gabby hanging out with Briggsey and his gang.

Ric closed the venetian blind and turned on his light. *Subject departed the premises at 21.17*, he wrote in his log under Gabby's name. *Subject wore dark clothing*. He flicked back over several pages, counting the times she'd been out since he started keeping the log. Seventeen times in about

six weeks. At first it had been only one night a week, then two, and now it was getting more and more frequent.

Matt Taylor, his closest friend, was the only one who knew about his log on Gabby. "Why bother?" Matt had wanted to know. "Are you going to tell on her? Or blackmail her or something?"

Twelve-hour time can be converted to 24-hour time by adding 12 to the hours after midday.

"Nah," Ric had replied. Although he wouldn't mind having something over Gabby; she was such a pain. "This is just practise. For when I'm going to be a detective."

"Oh." Matt immediately lost any interest. "Pity we couldn't stake out a real crime."

Ric mentally agreed, but real crimes weren't so easy to find. Oh sure, louts had broken the window of the shop a couple of times, but nothing more than that. Meanwhile he'd just have to practise on his family.

That night, he made himself stay awake

detective: *somebody whose job it is to uncover information and evidence about crimes and to discover who it was who committed a crime.*

until Gabby came back. Detectives didn't go to sleep on the job, he reminded himself whenever his eyes grew heavy. Actually she made it easy for him this time: she wasn't as quiet as usual. Ric jerked out of a semi-sleep when he heard the window slide all the way open.

Ric yawned, clicked on his bedside light and scribbled *Subject returned at 23.45 p.m.* on the notepad by his bed. Logging Gabby was getting boring. Who cared when she came in and out and met her deadhead friends? And he was missing sleep. In the morning, he decided, he was going to move on to a different branch of police procedure. Identification of suspects sounded interesting. He decided to start with his brother Tony.

The next morning Ric sat down opposite Tony at the breakfast table and watched while he wolfed down his cereal. Ric thought about identification of suspects. You were supposed to look for distinguishing features. How would someone describe Tony? Blond hair in that surfer's cut that Mum hated: all one length and never combed. But that didn't

Police procedures are the guidelines police must follow. The rules are there to protect the police in dangerous situations and to make sure the police behave properly.

really make him stand out. So what else?

Ric ran through the things that Detective Taylor had taught him. Anyone can change the colour of their hair or the way they dress, Ric, she'd told him. What you look for are the things they can't change. Tattoos. The shape of noses and ears. Any birthmarks or scars or flaws. Look for distinctive rings and jewellery too.

A disguise is anything that changes your appearance to hide your identity.

Ric chomped on a piece of toast and looked at Tony's ears. They stuck out a bit, but they weren't too bad. Ordinary bluey-grey eyes. His nose was like anyone else's too. So what could he describe about Tony that would help someone identify him? No tattoos; no scars…wait, yes, there was a scar.

Ric stopped chewing and narrowed his eyes, focussing on the small scar above Tony's right eye. Would that count? It was so small you could hardly see it. And Ric only knew it was there because he'd put it there in the first place. Although it was really Tony's fault for getting in the way when Ric had swung the bat.

Tony frowned at Ric. "What?" he asked. "Why are you staring at me?"

"I'm not staring." Ric continued eating

his toast, and took a swig of flavoured milk. Blast! He was sure real detectives didn't let people know that they were mentally making notes about what they looked like.

Tony up-ended his bowl and drank the last of the milk. "I'm going. Gotta meet Smacka at the surf." Tony got up, shrugged into his backpack and packed up his boogie board. "See you."

Ric shifted his attention to Gabby. She was staring moodily into her coffee, a sullen pout on her lips. "Hey, Gabs," he said. "You look cheerful this morning. Didn't sleep too well?"

She shot him a killing look. "I slept fine, nerd. Mind your own business."

"Oooh," he said, feigning fear. "Sorr-ee."

"Don't you two start," said his mother wearily. "Gabriella, I want you home right after school. It's your turn in the shop."

"The shop," Gabby spat. Her eyebrows drew together in a ferocious frown. "I never get to see my friends because of the shop. And why do I have to do more than they do?" She jerked her thumb in Ric's direction. He noticed she had a new ring on that hand.

When describing people, police note their height, build (slim, medium or solid), skin colour (dark, medium, light), age, colour and length of hair, and type of clothing.

A silver one. Mentally he made a note: *Subject wore a silver ring with wires twined together*. He frowned. That didn't sound right. Would you say "a woven-looking ring"? No, "intertwined", that was it. *Subject wore an intertwined silver ring.*

"You all put in the same amount of time," her mother said. "You know that. Don't make an issue of it. Ric did yesterday, Tony the day before."

Gabby shoved her chair back from the table and flounced over to the sink, banging down her cup. "Well, I'm sick of it." Her school uniform was hitched halfway up her thighs.

"Gabriella, lengthen that skirt. It looks cheap. I'm tired of telling you all the time."

Gabby gave a loud sigh. "Everybody wears their skirts like this."

"You're not leaving the house like that."

"Okay," said Gabby, smiling nastily. "Fine. I didn't want to go to school anyway."

"Here we go again," said Ric, and got up to leave.

"Shut up, nerd."

"Gabriella!"

Ric went to his room. If his mother

knew about Gabby's regular night trips in Briggsey's car, she wouldn't be so worried about a short uniform skirt. Or imagine if she spotted the navel-ring that everyone could see when Gabby wore her short-cropped tops with her jeans. Or the nose-ring...

Nose-ring and navel-ring! He picked up his detective notebook and wrote Gabby's name, then: *Subject sometimes wears a silver nose-ring and a silver navel-ring and has an intertwined silver ring on her right hand.* Yes, they were all good things to notice.

Then he heard Tony rush back into the house. "Mum! Mum!"

His brother's voice was urgent. Usually, once Tony headed off to the surf it would take a tidal wave to bring him back. What had happened? Ric hurried back to the kitchen.

"There's police car up the road at Mr Kent's house. And an ambulance too!" said Tony. Then he turned and ran back out as fast as he'd come in. They all followed him and stared up the road.

"Oh, my goodness." His mother put her hand up to her mouth. "I wonder what's happened?"

Many police cars have a number on the roof so that it can be identified by police aircraft.

"I'll go up and see," said Ric.

His mother frowned. "I don't know whether…well, all right." Ric could tell she wanted to know what had happened, but didn't want to seem like a stickybeak. "Don't get in the way."

Uniformed officers are usually first at the crime scene. Their job is to control crowds and make sure no unauthorised people, such as reporters, enter the scene.

Get in the way! As if she needed to tell him that. Honestly, his mother still treated him as though he was four, not twelve. Ric jogged up the road and across to join the small crowd at Mr Kent's front gate. A uniformed police officer was standing outside, telling them to keep back out of the way and leave room for the paramedics. Ric stared at the open front door. He hoped Mr Kent was okay. He went to stand next to Alicia, a kid in his class.

"What happened?" he asked her.

Alicia shrugged. "I don't know. I just got here."

Then the ambulance officers came through the door with the stretcher. Ric could hardly see Mr Kent. He had a tube going into his arm and an oxygen mask over his face. His eyes were closed, and he looked very white. There was a bandage round his head.

"Someone hit him," said Alicia,

nudging him. "Look at the bandage!"

Mr Kent was a nice old fellow. Ric, Tony and Gabby sometimes took him groceries to save him walking to the shop when his bad leg was giving him trouble.

"Did someone break in and bash him?"

Then another car pulled up. Matt's mother got out. She gave Ric a quick nod as she went past, then disappeared through the front door. So they had detectives on the job, thought Ric. What was going on?

The ambulance moved off down the road, siren blaring. That didn't sound good. If Mr Kent was all right, they'd just drive to the hospital without the siren, wouldn't they? Ric took a last look at the front door, which Matt's mother had closed behind her. He'd ask Matt later if he knew anything.

Everyone went back to their own houses. Ric told his mother and Gabby what he knew, which wasn't much.

Ric's mother shook her head. "The poor old man. How can people do that kind of thing? I'll find out more at the shop today. The word will get around." Even Gabby looked a bit shaken. She stared up the

Paramedics, who provide emergency medical attention, are allowed into a crime scene to attend to the injured. Police make a note of anything they touch.

Detectives are called in by uniformed police when a crime that has been committed requires investigation.

street at the police car, and bit her lip. "I'm going to school, Mum. I'm going to Suzi's place first, okay?"

His mother wasn't too keen on Suzi, so it was an indication of how upset she was that she didn't say anything. "All right, Gabriella. But fix your skirt."

Gabby ignored her and went inside for her things. Ric left too; he always got to Matt's early and had a second breakfast there, while he swapped jokes with Mr Taylor. There was plenty to talk about today. Here was real-life crime…but he didn't know if this was what he had wanted—something bad happening to someone he knew.

Unless…he could somehow help to find out who did it.

chapter 2

The first real case

WHEN HE ARRIVED at Matt's place, Mr Taylor and Matt were both sitting at the table eating omelettes. Mr Taylor was making "mmm…mmm" noises. He often did that about his own cooking.

"Hey, Ricardo!" said Mr Taylor, rolling his r's. He liked to think he sounded Italian when he said Ric's name. "Just in time for my super-duper new recipe for omelette."

"Oh, it's okay. I've eaten," said Ric. He always said that to be polite. And Mr Taylor always said, "I'm sure you can fit in another breakfast, being a growing boy!" or, as he did today, "Gotta fuel-up for the day—have another one!" He winked and moved to the stove, whistling.

Matt's family was the coolest. His mum was out a lot, at odd times, because of her job, but his dad was usually at home. He used to work in a bank, but he had taken some sort of payout a few years before. Now he ran a mail-order business from home. The garage was always stacked with heaps of boxes, and sometimes Ric and Matt earned extra money helping to pack orders.

As soon as Ric sat down, Matt was full of the news. "Hey, you'll never guess where Mum had to go this morning!"

"Wanna bet?" Ric took the orange juice that Mr Taylor set down in front of him. "I saw her go into Mr Kent's place. They took him away in an ambulance. What happened?"

"Robbery and GBH, they said." Matt scraped up the last mouthful of omelette and swallowed. "Looks like he got bashed when he disturbed them. A home invasion."

"He was always nice to us," Ric said to Matt. "Remember, he gave us those biscuits when we took the groceries round there last week?"

GBH: *Grievous Bodily Harm, a serious form of physically attacking someone.*

Mr Taylor whisked eggs and scraped finely chopped bacon and herbs into the mixture. "She'll find them, guys, don't you worry. She's good at her job. And most crims slip up sooner or later." He looked over at Ric. "Did you know him well, Ric?"

Ric shrugged. "Pretty well. All our family did, because he's been coming to the shop for years. And we've all dropped in groceries for him. He was always nice." He took another sip of juice. "I wish we could do something. Like ask questions around, you know? See if anyone's heard anything."

"No harm in keeping your ears open," said Mr Taylor, emptying the mixture into the sizzling pan. "But don't start asking questions that might get you into trouble, Ric. There's some pretty dicey characters hanging around that shopping complex where you've got your supermarket."

Ric thought about that. He knew that Mr Taylor was right. Someone had hurled a brick through the shop window once before, when his father had called the police about a fight going on out the front. He didn't want the same thing to happen again.

"We'll be careful," he promised. "But everyone'll be talking about this in our street anyway." He looked over at Matt's dad. "Mr Taylor…?"

"Yep?" He turned to look at Ric, shaking the omelette pan over a low flame.

"What do the police do first when something like this happens?"

Mr Taylor had heard his wife talk about enough cases to have a fair idea of what went on. "Find out what they can from the victim, if he can talk. See if they can get a description. Then I think they'll ask the neighbours if they heard or saw anything." He flipped the omelette. "Might be better if you asked Linda when she comes home. You guys are always talking detective stuff, right?" He shot Ric a smile over his shoulder.

While Matt packed his bag, Ric finished the omelette and thought about what he could do next. He knew a lot of the kids that came into his family's shop. He could talk to them this afternoon. He could hang around outside and muck about on his skateboard—it was Gabby's turn to help out behind the counter. He could ask everybody if they knew anyone who came regularly to Mr Kent's home.

That wouldn't be asking for trouble, would it? He could just say that he was wondering who Mr Kent's friends were, so they could make sure they knew that Mr Kent was in hospital. He was sure he could ask questions without letting on that he and Matt were investigating the case.

Wow! This was his first real case! Okay, so he wasn't a detective yet—but he could be a private detective, couldn't he? Everyone had to start somewhere.

Matt came out. "Ready to go?"

Ric jumped up. "Sure. Let's go." He was ready to go all right. Ready to go and to start asking questions. He and Matt could solve this case!

An identikit is used to create a portrait from the description of a suspect given to the police by the victim or witness. This is a police identikit image of Margaret McAlister, the author of this book.

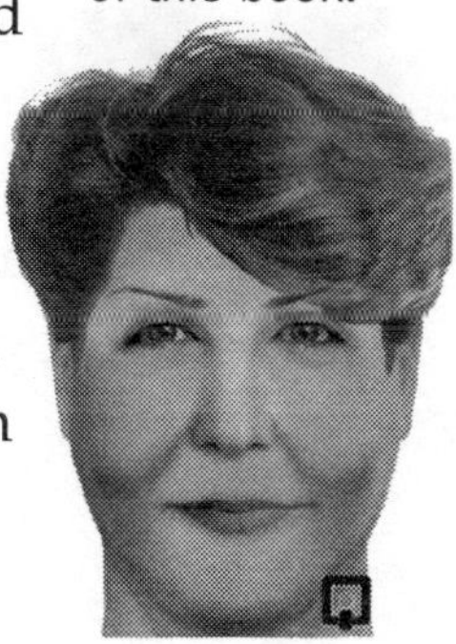

Ric persuaded Matt to work with him on the case. They agreed to find out as much as they could from Matt's mother. Late that afternoon, Matt rang to tell him that she was home. Ric arrived at Matt's less than ten minutes later.

Matt let him in. "She's in the kitchen," he said. "Reading the paper and talking to Dad."

"Is she in a good mood?"

"Okay, I think. She's been talking to Dad about Mr Kent. I heard her say that if he dies, whoever did it will be charged with murder."

They walked into the kitchen. Matt's dad was standing at the hotplates, stirring pasta. Tonight he was wearing a bright green apron with a huge frog's face on it, with a message under it saying, "Kissed Any Frogs Today?"

"Hi, Mr Taylor," said Ric, grinning. "Does that mean you want me to kiss you?"

"You volunteering? If you were a good-looking blonde maybe."

"In your dreams," said Matt's mum, who was tall and skinny with red frizzy hair. She closed her newspaper. "Hi, guys. What gives?"

"Hi, Detective," said Ric. "Solved any crimes today?"

It was his usual greeting to Matt's mum. Ever since she'd found out he wanted to be a detective she'd jokingly called him "Detective Ric", and he usually returned the greeting. He could still remember the day he'd known he wanted to be a detective. It was a Saturday, and for a change Matt's mother had been free to pick up Ric and take him and Matt to their soccer game. It was usually Matt's dad who drove them to the games, because Ric's parents were always at the shop.

On the way, Matt's mum started talking about the role of forensic science in policing. As Ric listened to what she had to say about preserving a crime scene and how a single fibre could lead to the conviction of the criminal, he felt a kind of excitement. Imagine tiny fibres that you could only see under a microscope helping to pinpoint a killer! Or a hair identifying a suspect.

Since then Ric had been finding out more and more about police work. Now he knew lots about it. And maybe, with Mr Kent's case, he could do some detecting himself. Matt's mother never told him much about the cases she was working on, but she often told him other interesting stuff. Today, she looked grim.

"I'd like to get the low-lifes who did over Ronald Kent," she said. "But we'll

forensic: *to do with the law courts.*

get them. Like I've told you lots of times, Ric—most criminals make mistakes."

"Is he going to die?"

"He's not too well, that's for sure. Could go either way."

Ric sat down on the next chair. "What will happen to the people who did it if he dies?"

"It'll be a murder charge," she said. "This is a serious crime. But let's hope it doesn't come to that."

"How will you find them?"

She looked at him and crossed her arms. She gave him what he called "That Look". Probably the one she gave crooks when she was telling them off. A kind of flat, lifeless stare. "Well, now, Detective, don't you remember anything I've taught you? Fine forensic detective you'll make."

Ric sat up straight in the chair. He hoped he could remember everything. "Yeah, I do. First you go in and look at the crime scene. And you don't touch anything."

"Right," she said. "Hands behind your back. Or in your pockets."

"You draw a diagram of where the body is, if there's a body," Ric went on. "And you look at everything and make

Police don't actually draw a chalk outline of a body at a murder scene, as is sometimes seen on TV.

notes, and the Crime Scene people come in and take photographs."

"Not bad," she said. "What else?"

"You dust for fingerprints." He looked at her and decided to push his luck. "Did you find any fingerprints at Mr Kent's place?"

"Now, Ric," she said, grinning. "You know I can't discuss a case. Let's talk basic procedure here."

"Okay." He thought about everything she'd told him and all the stuff in his books about forensic science and detection. "You go to see all the neighbours and ask if they heard or saw anything suspicious, or if they've seen any different cars around and all that stuff. And you ask them to call you if they remember anything."

"No matter how small," she agreed.

"And you find out who knows Mr Kent, and if anyone's been in his house recently, like tradesmen or visitors. And if he's got any enemies. And one interview leads to another."

The Crime Scene Unit collects evidence from where the crime took place. This could be tyre marks, fingerprints, blood specimens, fibres or hairs. Some evidence may be sent to a forensic laboratory for further analysis.

CRIME SCENE – DO NOT CROSS

Neighbours are a good source of information. They often notice unusual activity.

"That's right," she said. "And don't forget the uniformed police will have already checked likely points of entry and taken note of who had been at the crime scene, and what they might have touched. Okay, you've passed today's exam, Detective. It's basically a lot of legwork. And a bit of thinking. Putting together the puzzle. Figuring out the likely suspects." She unfolded her arms and stabbed a finger at him. "You, for example, are a suspect in this case."

Ric's mouth dropped open. He stared at her. "What?" Was she joking? How could he be a suspect? Sure, he knew Mr Kent, but so did half the neighbourhood. So did Matt!

Matt laughed. He punched Ric on the arm. "All right, confess. Where were you last night?"

Ric could tell Matt's mum was serious. Well, he was sure she didn't actually suspect him. She knew him too well for that...didn't she? But what did she mean? Matt's mother tilted one red eyebrow at him. "Think about it."

Ric hadn't thought for one moment that

alibi: *proof of being elsewhere at the time a crime was committed.*

he'd need an alibi. He swallowed hard. "I was at home," he said. "Watching television. And then I went to bed." Actually, he had been sort of awake listening to his CDs for hours, waiting to complete his log on Gabby, but he didn't want to tell Matt's mother that. She'd probably think he was going a bit too far. He frowned. "I suppose I could have climbed out of the window. But so could Matt. So could half the kids we hang out with!"

"True," she said. "Keep thinking." Ric sat racking his brain. Why was he a suspect more than the others? He went over what he'd already told her. Crime scene. Fingerprints. He hadn't been there, so his fingerprints couldn't be—

His fingerprints. They might be there, because he delivered groceries sometimes. In fact, he'd taken groceries to Mr Kent the day before he'd been attacked. He'd gone right into the kitchen. And sat on a chair drinking a lemonade.

"You've got my fingerprints," he said. "From when I took him his groceries."

"We could well have," she agreed. "But we wouldn't know, because your

Fingerprints are patterns on the skin of fingertips. No two people have exactly the same pattern. When police arrest someone, they take a record of their fingerprints (see page 91–92). These can then be checked to see if they match fingerprints found at crime scenes.

Different parts of fingerprints have distinct features. These are analysed by fingerprint experts. There are three main features of fingerprints: arches, loops, and whorls.

fingerprints are not on file. But you're on the right track. You've been in the house—several times. And you know what he's got in there. Video, television. You know the layout, don't you, Ric?"

The room was silent. Ric felt the blood draining from his face. He swallowed. He looked at Matt, who was looking thoughtful. He looked at Matt's mother, who was staring at him with that flat-eyed look again. He felt a shiver go through him.

"Yeah," he said. "I guess I do."

"Well, there you go, then," she said. "You see? There are probably lots of people who could be suspects." She grinned at him, and became just Matt's mum again. He couldn't believe how quickly she could change. He wondered if she did that with suspects. "Lots of people go in there for one reason or another. There's a local nurse who calls around from time to time to dress his bad leg. And there's Meals on Wheels. And his gardener."

Ric felt deflated. "Well, how are you going to find them, then? If there are so many people who could have done it?"

"The video's missing," she said. "So's

his television and a little CD player. They could turn up somewhere, and that'll give us another lead. They might be sold in a pub, or they might turn up at one of those cash advance places. We've got ways of checking. And people talk. One way or another, we'll find out."

She folded the paper in front of her, and pointed a finger at Ric. "Be careful, Ric. I know you liked Mr Kent. But asking questions can get you into trouble. Let the police deal with this."

"But I can keep my ears open," Ric said, remembering Mr Taylor's words that morning. "And pass on anything I hear to you…right?"

"Right, Detective." She winked. "Listening is a highly underrated activity. Keep quiet, listen and it's amazing what you can pick up. And if you do find out something, let me know right away. Okay?"

Ric nodded. He knew just what he was going to do next. Go and hang out at the shop. It was open for another couple of hours, and the gangs would be gathering. He might ask Gabby to keep her ears open, too. There was information out there. And he was going to find it.

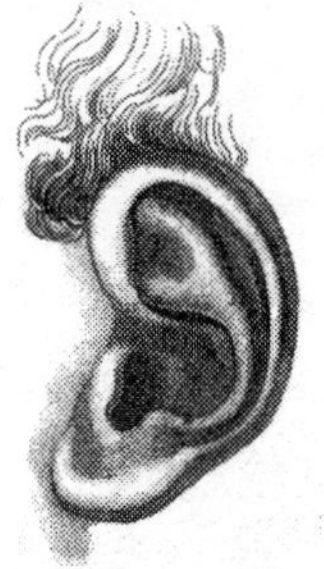

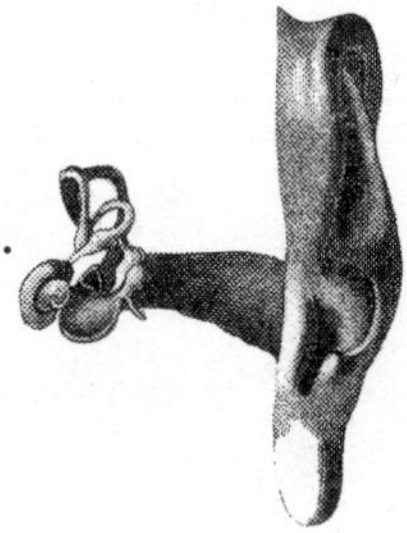

The ear is formed in such a way that the vibrations produced by any sound can be picked up and transmitted to the ear drum. People usually hear more if they concentrate on listening.

chapter 3

Hanging out at the shop

RIC AND MATT rounded the corner on their skateboards and rode downhill to the shop. The usual groups of kids were hanging around. Jason Conroy and his gang were leaning against the wall between the fish and chip shop and Ric's shop. Kevin Johnson and Peter Budiansky were doing skateboard tricks using the gutter in front of the video shop. No sign of Briggsey yet, but his friend Chris Papandreou was already there, leaning on the bonnet of a souped-up Ford.

Ric and Matt skated up to Kevin and Peter. "How's it going?" said Ric.

"Hey, man!" Kevin leaned back on his board to stop it. The four of them moved over to sit on the low stone wall that divided the five shops in the complex from the parking lot. Ric looked around. Would any of these kids know anything? He wasn't sure how to start. He had to lead the conversation around to Mr Kent, without being too obvious.

For a few minutes the four of them talked about school and the movie they all wanted to see, then Ric had an idea. He got up. "I'll be back in a minute," he said. "I just want to ask my mum if she's heard anything about how Mr Kent is." Ric looked at Kevin and Peter. "He lives near our place. He got bashed and robbed this morning." Then he glanced at Matt to see if he'd understood the message: keep talking about the subject while he was gone. Matt scratched his nose, a code between them meaning "Okay, I got it."

Ric wandered into the shop. Gabby was ringing up a purchase for a woman with two whining kids hanging onto her. "No," the woman snapped at them. "You can't have a chocolate frog, and that's that."

One of the kids started to cry. Gabby glared at the kid, gave the woman some change,

Stolen goods can be identified by serial numbers, a photographic record, or if the owner has engraved a code or number onto them

then shoved her bread, milk and cookies into a bag and pushed it across the counter. "Here." Without waiting for the woman to leave, she said to Ric, "Do me a favour? Stand in for me for a while? Just five minutes."

"Sorry," said Ric. "I've got things to do. Gotta see Mum." He knew Gabby wanted to go outside and talk to Chris and Evania Papandreou. And sneak a cigarette, if she thought her mother wasn't looking. Too bad: it was Gabby's day in the shop.

"Creep!" Gabby called after him as he walked down to the back of the store where his mother was stacking the shelves. "Five minutes wouldn't have killed you!"

Ric ignored her. He squatted next to his mother and started to help her stack boxes on the shelf. "Mum, have you heard anything more about Mr Kent?"

"Ricardo." She gave him a tired smile. "What are you doing here? Have you done your homework?"

"I don't have any tonight. Have you heard anything?"

"A little. Not much. Kath from next door to him came in. She's had the police in asking questions. She didn't hear anything, she said, but it looks like they were stealing his television and video when he heard them and got up. Foolish man! Why didn't he just call the police?" She shook her head and handed him more boxes. "Kath thinks his grandson Ray might know something. I hope not. But he was a wild boy a few years ago; everyone knew about him."

Neighbourhood Watch is a program designed to combat crime by encouraging neighbours to keep an eye on each other's property.

Ric nodded thoughtfully. He knew that from talking to Detective Taylor. She'd taken Ric along to a Neighbourhood Watch meeting one night when she was talking about home security. She'd talked about deadlocks, keeping bushes trimmed near the house and watching for any suspicious activity in neighbouring houses. She'd told a story about how one lot of thieves hired a removalist's truck and took the whole house full of furniture. The neighbours just thought that the people must have decided to move house without telling anyone, so didn't do anything. When the home-owners came back from holidays, they found an empty house.

Matt's mother had also talked about what to do if you hear noises in the house and realise that you have a burglar. *Don't try to do anything,* she said. *Don't try to be a hero. That's a good way to get killed. Phone the police from an extension, or on a mobile phone. Or go to the neighbour's place and phone from there. If you can, take the registration plate of a car. But don't try to do anything.*

Poor Mr Kent. He'd tried to stop them. And look what happened to him. "Have you heard how Mr Kent is?" he asked his mother.

"Yes, I phoned the hospital. He hasn't regained consciousness yet." She shook her head and stopped him before he put down the next box. "Ric, remember what I told you, put the latest use-by dates at the back of the shelf. Otherwise we lose money."

Police recommend that you do not confront an intruder. If possible, phone the police and tell them there is someone in the house.

"Sorry." He changed the order of the boxes. "But if he disturbed them and they hit him, how did he ring the police?"

"He didn't. Kath Conroy next door has a spare key, because he has trouble with his leg and he's fallen a few times. If she doesn't see him around, she phones him to check. Then if he doesn't answer, she goes in. She found him lying there." She sighed. "Kath feels guilty because she didn't hear anything, but why would you? Normal people go to sleep in the middle of the night."

Ric nodded. "I'm going back outside to ride my skatie for a while. Unless you need any help?" He hoped she'd say no.

"No, I've almost finished."

Ric stood up. "See you at home then."

Luckily Gabby was busy with a line of people at the counter, so she had no time to do anything but throw him a sulky look as he squeezed past. Ric gave her a wave and grinned.

Outside, Matt was still sitting on the wall. Kevin and Peter were visible down near the bottom of the road, weaving complicated-looking circles on their boards.

"You get anything from them?" Ric asked.

"They didn't even know he got hurt," said Matt. "What'd your mum say?"

Ric told him, and they sat and thought about the next move. "This detective business isn't as easy as you'd think," he said. "You can't do much as a private detective, can you? We can't look at fingerprints. We can't look at the crime scene. We can't knock on doors and ask

Private detectives do not have access to the information on police databases.

people what they saw. Well, we can, but they don't have to tell us."

Matt snickered. "I don't think people are going to answer questions from kids. Anyway, the police are already doing that. We have to think of what we can do."

About the only people they could talk to were other kids, Ric thought, but kids didn't know much. He looked over at Chris Papandreou. He was sitting inside his car now, sideways behind the steering wheel, with his feet resting on the ground outside. Loud music throbbed from his car. His sister Evania was sitting on the bonnet. She was wearing tight blue jeans and a short black top. The sun glinted on

interview: *formally arranged questioning of a person.*

something on her stomach. Ric squinted at her. She had a navel-ring like Gabby. They'd probably had it done at the same time.

Then he had a brainwave. Gabby would be able to find out more from them than he could. Even if they did know anything, they wouldn't tell him. Maybe he could work out a swap with Gabby: do half an hour behind the counter for her if she agreed to ask them if they knew anything. She'd probably agree: she'd be so glad to get out for a while.

Gabby looked at him as though he was mad. "Ask my friends if they know anything about Mr Kent being robbed? You've got to be kidding. How would they know anything?"

Ric didn't think it would be tactful to say that she hung around with a bunch of losers, and if anyone knew anything it would be them. So he just said "Look, they probably don't know anything, all right? But you never know. They might have heard someone talking. They might know of someone trying to sell a stolen TV."

"You're nuts." Gabby put her hands on her hips. "Always trying to be the little

Criminals, or people who associate with criminals, who regularly give information to the police are called informants.

Witnesses or informants are sometimes unwilling to give information because of threats of violence.

detective, aren't you? Think you're smart hanging around with that Matt and his dorky detective mother." Her face darkened. "You're just a kid. You don't know anything."

"Well, I know a lot more than you," said Ric, stung. "You think you're so smart, sneaking out at night the way you do. I know what you do. I've been keeping a surveillance log.

Gabby's face went white, then red. She leaned forward and grabbed him by the shirt. "You sneaky little creep! Spying on me! So help me, if you say anything—" Suddenly she seemed to remember where she was, and hurriedly scanned the shop to see if her mother was listening. When she saw her mother was busy in the back room, she turned her attention back to Ric. "You say one word—one word—and I'll tell Briggsey. He'll soon fix you."

Ric swallowed. Having Briggsey "fix him" was the last thing he wanted. "Okay, okay. I wasn't going to say anything. How about a deal? You go and ask Chris and Evania if they know anything, and I'll keep quiet."

"You'd better," she spat at him. "I'm warning you—"

"Okay, okay! I said I wouldn't tell." He moved around behind the counter. "All you have to do is ask if they've heard anything about who might have done it. And I'll do half an hour for you here."

She looked at him, her eyes narrowed into slits. "You'd better not say anything to Mum."

"I won't." He pointed at his watch. "Half an hour."

Gabby was still mad. "The rest of the day. You owe me for spying on me."

"No." When he wanted to, Ric could be just as stubborn as his sister. "You owe me for not telling. Half an hour. And I'll be coming out."

"All right." Gabby pushed past him, elbowing him in the ribs. "Creep."

Ric watched her leave. He had an uncomfortable feeling in his chest. Would she really tell Briggsey? He groaned. Why had he told her what he'd been doing?

To Ric's surprise, Gabby was back in exactly half an hour.

"Well?" he asked, when there was no-one else within earshot. "What did you find out?"

"Nothing." She curled her lip at him,

Stolen goods are often sold in places such as markets where thieves don't have to provide identification or proof of ownership.

her dark eyes unfriendly. "I told you my friends wouldn't know anything. They haven't heard about any attack."

"I didn't think they would know about the attack," Ric tried to explain. "I just thought they might have heard about a TV or video being for sale—"

"So they hang out with thieves? Is that what you're saying?"

Ric gave up. It was impossible to reason with Gabby. Life would be a lot simpler if he didn't have a sister. At least this sister. "Okay, thanks anyway. See you later."

"And don't spy on me ever again!"

Outside, Ric met up with Matt—only to find that he hadn't had any luck at all. Apparently Gabby had come storming out of the shop, talked fast to Chris and Evania Papandreou while waving her arms around a lot, then the whole lot of them piled into the car and took off. When she came back she went straight into the shop. "I couldn't hear anything she said," explained Matt apologetically. "The skateboard was making too much noise. I couldn't stop and listen, could I? It would have looked a bit obvious."

So, Gabby had been furious and waving her arms around? Ric felt a sinking feeling in his stomach. He knew Gabby in that mood. She must have been telling them about him spying on her. And if Chris Papandreou knew, it wouldn't be long before Briggsey knew.

He was dead.

chapter 4

The crime scene

THE NEXT DAY was Saturday, and Ric was anxious to keep out of Briggsey's way. "Why don't we go and see Mrs Conroy?" he suggested to Matt. "You know, the lady who lives next door to Mr Kent?"

At just after ten-thirty, they were knocking on Mrs Conroy's door. She opened it and stood there with wet pink plastic gloves on. She looked pleased to see them. "Oh good, Ric," she said. Most of the people around knew Ric because he worked in the shop so much. "Come in, I'm washing the dog. You can help hold her for me."

Ric and Matt followed her through to the back verandah. "I didn't know you had a dog."

"I don't. She's Ronald Kent's dog. I'm looking after her while he's in hospital."

Ric bent down and patted Daisy, a tiny little terrier. Right now, soaked with water and huddling in a corner of the verandah, she looked more like a large rat than a dog. She licked Ric eagerly. He had often played with her when he took stuff round to Mr Kent from the shop.

"Poor Daisy," he said. "Don't you like bath time?" He picked her up and gently plunged her in the waiting tub of water. He quickly soaped her with flea shampoo, taking care not to get it in her eyes. "Not much of a watchdog, were you, Dais?"

"You got that right," said Mrs Conroy. "Poor old bloke. I told him before, living on his own like that, he needed a big dog. Something like a German shepherd or a rottie."

Ric shivered. He'd been bitten by a rottweiler once. They might make good guard dogs, but he preferred Daisy. "I just came to see if you'd heard anything more about Mr Kent," he said. "Is he conscious yet?" He rinsed the soap off Daisy, and wrapped her in the old towel Matt held out.

"No. The hospital won't tell you much, if you're not a relative. But I was talking

Sometimes a dog on the premises can stop burglars from trying to break in.

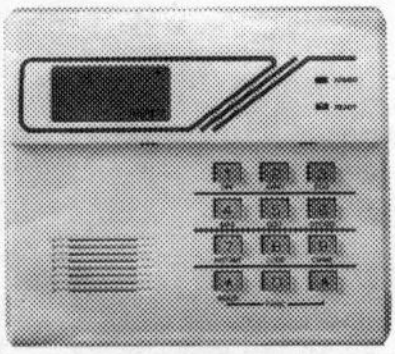

There are different types of alarms. Most need a code keyed-in to turn them on or off.

to his daughter, Maxine, when I said I'd take care of the dog. She said he's looking bad. Took a turn for the worse overnight, apparently." Mrs Conroy shook her head. "If I hadn't seen the milk sitting out in the sun, he could have died before anyone knew."

Ric rubbed Daisy dry, then let her go. He watched while she bounded off down the yard and rolled in the grass. Dogs were so weird.

"I tell you what, it's made me determined to do something to protect myself," said Mrs Conroy. "It could have been me, I told that detective lady. She said I should get an alarm. The Neighbourhood Watch have a leaflet about a good one that doesn't cost too much. And window locks."

"It's a wonder she didn't have you putting in smoke detectors as well," said Matt with a grin. "She usually talks people into all those things."

"Detective Taylor is Matt's mum," Ric explained, jerking a thumb in his friend's direction.

"Is she now?" Mrs Conroy looked at Matt with renewed interest. "Doesn't miss a trick that one, I'd say. She left here with a list of people to interview."

"Did she?" asked Ric. "Like who?"

"Oh, nobody much. Nobody who would have done this," she said. "Just people who came to the house regularly. The nurse, the gardener, his daughter and grandson." She snorted. "Wouldn't put anything past that grandson, though. Probably a druggie."

"And then there's you and your sister and your brother," Mrs Conroy went on, looking at Ric. "Not that I think your family would do this, Ric. I don't think you can put this down to anyone who comes to the house regularly, except maybe that grandson of his. I think it was just bad luck that someone chose his house."

Ric nodded. "Mum said you were the one who called the police."

"Yes, that's right." Mrs Conroy stripped off the plastic gloves and laid them over the railing. "You should have seen the poor old feller. Gave me a right turn, it did, to see him lying there like that, hardly breathing, with blood on the floor under his head. I rang the emergency number right away. Good thing the ambulance came as quickly as it did.

In most countries there is a special emergency telephone number. The operator will ask which service you need: police, ambulance or fire brigade.

Tyre tread leaves marks on various surfaces which can be used to help prove that a particular vehicle was present at a crime scene.

They said he'd been lying there half the night."

"And you didn't hear a thing?"

"Nothing different to usual. There are always kids roaring around here in cars, with the shopping centre so close. You know what it's like."

Ric knew, all right. There were black tyre marks permanently burnt into the road surface outside their supermarket. Every night kids met there, after the shops had closed, to do burn-offs in their cars, and race around the neighbouring streets. They didn't do it so often now that new laws had been brought in, and police could confiscate their cars. He gave a short laugh at the thought of Briggsey or Chris Papandreou having their cars impounded. They'd freak.

He looked across at Mr Kent's house next door. "Mum said you have a spare key."

"Yeah, that's right. Good thing, too."

Ric hesitated. "Could you show us where it happened? And what's been taken?"

She frowned. "Well, now, I don't like poking around in people's houses when they're not there. And I don't think the police would like it either. They've been in there taking fingerprints and the like. I don't know if they're finished yet. I'd better not."

"Okay." She was looking at him a bit suspiciously, so Ric thought he'd better explain. "It's just we told Matt's mum we'd keep our ears open, see, and I want to be a detective one day too, and I thought it'd be interesting to have a look at the crime scene. But don't worry. Sorry."

Mrs Conroy looked across at the house next door. "Crime scene, eh? I didn't think of it like that, but I suppose it is." She hesitated again. "Well, I had to go in to get Daisy's basket and her bowl, so I suppose you could come in and have a quick look. But no poking around, mind."

"Don't worry," said Matt. "We know what to do at a crime scene."

Mrs Conroy laughed. "Oh, you do, do you? All right then. Come on."

She went back to the kitchen to get a key, then led the way down the side path of Mr Kent's house. Daisy bounded along in front of everyone, still looking a bit damp and bedraggled.

Once inside, Ric looked at the familiar

Records of fingerprints are kept on computer in the Automated Fingerprint Identification System. Prints found at a crime scene can be speedily identified if they belong to a known law breaker.

kitchen and lounge room with new eyes. He immediately saw the blank spot where the television had been. On the shelf underneath it was a square imprint where the video used to be. Black powder was all over the place: on the door handles, on the furniture and on the backs of the kitchen chairs. That was for fingerprints, of course, he knew that much.

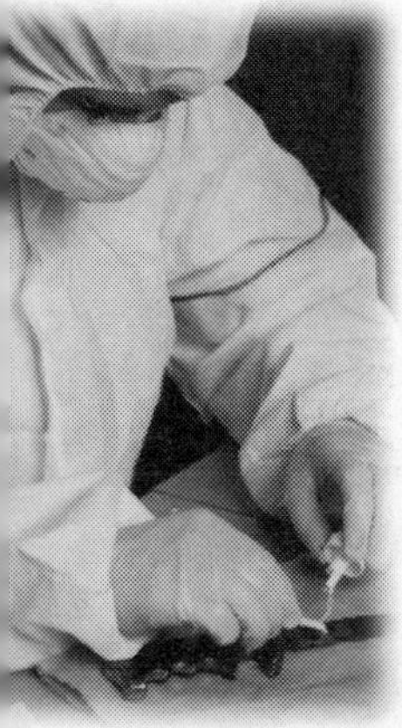

Forensic scientists sometimes wear protective clothing when examining evidence. This is to ensure they do not contaminate it.

There was a patch of dried blood on the carpet near the coffee table. His stomach rolled. He pointed at the stain. "Is that where you found him?"

Mrs Conroy sighed. "Yes, poor man."

Ric wandered a few steps into the kitchen. The small portable CD player had gone from the kitchen table. Mr Kent didn't have much for them to steal.

"We'd better go," said Mrs Conroy. "Grab that dog dish on the floor there, Ric." She opened a cupboard and took out some cans of dog food. "And get her basket from the laundry."

Within five minutes, they were out of there, carrying Daisy's belongings. And on the way out, they ran into someone coming in through the gate. Someone dressed in a black T-shirt with holes in it.

Someone with a nose-stud and four or five ear-rings in each ear.

Ric didn't need to look at Mrs Conroy's tightened lips to guess who this was. The grandson. Could he be guilty? Would he attack his own grandfather?

"Hello Ray," Mrs Conroy said in a voice that didn't sound at all friendly. "I've just been in to pick up Daisy's things. Have you seen your grandfather this morning?"

"Yeah, I've been over to the hospital with Mum." Ray gave her an equally unfriendly look. "No change."

Ric had no doubts at all that Ray knew exactly what Mrs Conroy thought of him. No wonder he wasn't bothering to chat. Should Ric try to talk to him? What could he say?

"We've just given Daisy a bath," he said. "And picked up her things."

Ray looked down at the dog. "Mum doesn't like dogs in the house. Daisy's not bad, I s'pose, but she's not big enough to frighten anyone away."

Ric and Matt exchanged glances. Ray would have known that Daisy couldn't protect anybody. Daisy would probably just wag her tail if Ray entered the house, since she was used to him coming to visit now and again. Yes, it was possible that Ray was the culprit.

But he might not be. Ric knew from his reading about psychopaths and sociopaths that there were lots of people who could seem nice but who were actually killers. Like Ted Bundy in America.

"See you," said Ray to the boys. He ignored Mrs Conroy. "I've got to pick up some pyjamas for Grandpa." He walked past them and went around the back.

Deadlocks can be locked with a key from the inside as well as the outside. If a burglar breaks in through a window, say, they cannot then take goods out the door.

"We'd better go," said Ric. "But we can come back and take Daisy for a walk later, if you want."

"Would you?" Mrs Conroy cast a meaningful look in Ray's direction. It was the sort of look that said she thought he should have been the one doing it. "Daisy'd like that. Thanks, Ric." She nodded to them and went inside.

Ric looked at Matt. "Now what? We didn't find out much from the crime scene."

Ric looked down the street towards his house, and thought how close he lived to Mr Kent. Anybody was at risk, really. His family didn't have deadlocks or an alarm or a dog. And look how easily Gabby had climbed in and out of the window. A burglar could do that, too.

"We could find out who the gardener is," said Matt. "But the police will already have interviewed him. There's no point us following him or anything. And he won't talk to us."

"Come back to my place," suggested Ric. "Let's look through my crime books. Maybe we'll get an idea from those."

The two of them set off down the road towards Ric's house. They were about two houses away when they heard the sound of a car coming up behind them. Ric's stomach clenched. He knew that sound.

He turned around just as the big black car throbbed to a stop beside them.

Briggsey. With Gabby in the seat beside him.

He got out. "Hey," he said, stabbing an ominous looking finger at Ric. "Come here. I want a word with you."

chapter 5

Quit asking questions

RIC FELT HIS PULSE speed up. He tried to look puzzled. "Me?"

"Yeah, you." Briggsey stepped up over the gutter and leaned on the bonnet of the car next to Gabby's window. "Come here."

Ric took a step closer. "What do you want?" He could feel his legs trembling, and hoped it didn't show.

Briggsey switched his attention to Matt. "You! Take off."

"Go on, Matt," said Ric without looking at him. "Wait for me in my room. I'll be there in a minute."

Matt hesitated, then jogged off down the street. Briggsey waited until he'd disappeared into Ric's driveway, then lowered his eyebrows and stared at Ric from underneath them. He took out a pack of cigarettes and took his time lighting one. *He's trying to scare me,* Ric thought. Matt's mother had told him about techniques police used in interviews to get the results they wanted. They could be tough and scare people. They could be soft and understanding. Briggsey was being tough.

The worst thing was, it was working. Ric watched him shake out the match slowly and toss it on the ground. Then he inhaled slowly and blew out a puff of smoke right in Ric's face. Ric managed not to cough.

"Gabby tells me you've been spying on her," said Briggsey. He waited.

Ric shot Gabby a foul look. "Anyone could hear her climbing in and out," he said. "She's not too quiet about it."

"And you followed her and saw her get in my car."

Ric shrugged. No point denying it. "Only once."

"You say anything to anyone, and there's not going to be much left of you. Understand?" Briggsey pushed himself off the car and took a step forward. He grabbed Ric's T-shirt and dragged him right up close until he was glaring into

There is no set interview procedure used by police. They vary the questioning technique depending on the situation and the individual.

Ric's eyes. His breath stank of cigarettes. He had a red, angry-looking pimple right next to his nose, and one of his two front teeth was chipped on one corner. "Understand?"

"I already told Gabby I wasn't going to say anything," gasped Ric. "Let me go!"

"One word, and I'm coming after you. Gabby doesn't want to be stuck at home or in that stinking shop any more than she is now. Just remember that." Briggsey shook him hard, then shoved him backwards. "And quit asking questions about how much we all know about the robbery. We don't know a thing. If we hear that you've been saying we do, you'll end up worse off than that old man. Remember that." He flicked his cigarette at Ric, and sauntered back around to the driver's side of the car.

Common assault can be actual physical contact or a verbal threat made by someone who is close enough to the victim to actually go through with physical assault.

Ric looked at Gabby. She had a smug smile on her face. He glared at her, but she just sneered and turned away. She leant over towards Briggsey as he got into the car, and that's when Ric saw the tattoo. Gabby was wearing a singlet top that scooped down at the back, and just below her left shoulder blade there was a tattoo of a smiling red devil. A sort of little cartoon devil, holding a pitchfork. Ric could see a tip of a forked tail curling up above the black singlet.

A devil. It pretty well summed up Gabby and her general attitude. She didn't care about the shop or his family or anything—only that dumb Briggsey.

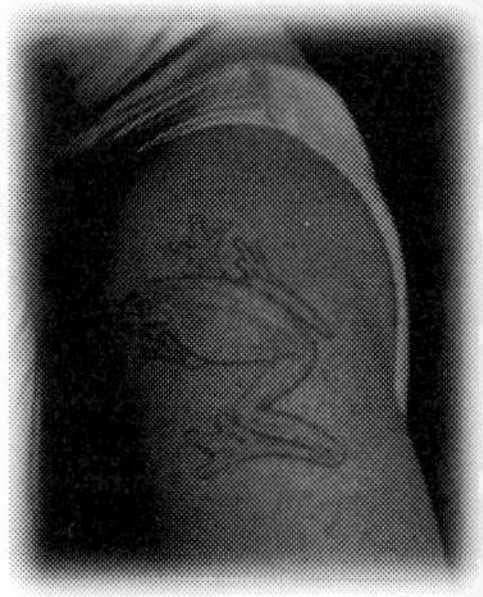

Tattoos are distinctive markings that can be used to identify a person.

With a throaty roar, the black Holden took off up the road. Ric automatically noted the licence plate. He'd been training himself to do that: to recognise cars and remember licence plates. Briggsey's car had a sunroof and mag wheels. On the back window, there was a sticker on the back saying "If you can read this you're too close".

He picked up a stick on the ground and threw it ahead as far as he could in frustration. Fat lot of good it would do to memorise Briggsey's licence plate. The cops would have written it down heaps of times, the way Briggsey roared around in that car.

Matt came out to meet him. "What did he want?"

"Just to scare me off. Warned me not to tell on Gabby. Not to ask questions about what he and his gang were doing last night." Ric kicked at the ground. "I'm about ready to give up. We'll never find out anything. Grown-ups don't want to talk to us. What's the use?"

"Hey, kid—" came a voice behind them.

Ric nearly jumped out of his skin. He whipped around, and saw Ray Kent a few steps behind them, carrying a plastic shopping bag. He looked just as frightening as Briggsey, with his short spiky hair and black T-shirt.

"You okay?" asked Ray. "You looked in a spot of trouble back there."

"I'm all right. Thanks." Ric took a long, slow breath.

Ray looked at him. "I know Steven Briggs," he said. "He's a bad man to cross. You be careful." He shifted the shopping bag to the other hand. Ric could see striped material through the thin plastic. Mr Kent's pyjamas. "Anyway, gotta go." He nodded and kept walking.

"He doesn't seem so bad to me," said Matt.

"Who knows?" said Ric. "Well, what are we going to do now? Give up? Leave it to the police?"

> Features used to identify a car include: the licence plate, make of vehicle, colour, style of car (sedan, station wagon, etc) and design extras (for example, mag wheels, racing stripes).

Matt shrugged. "Do what we were going to do. Look at your crime books. Maybe they'll give us an idea."

For an hour, they looked through books and talked crime. Ric was surprised to find how many books he had collected. There was one that was based on a television series. It showed how the crime scene told a story to the police so they were able to track down the people responsible. Usually, the crime scene gave more than one clue—hairs, fibres, imprints of weapons used, and spatter patterns for bloodstains that told police a lot about how a crime was committed.

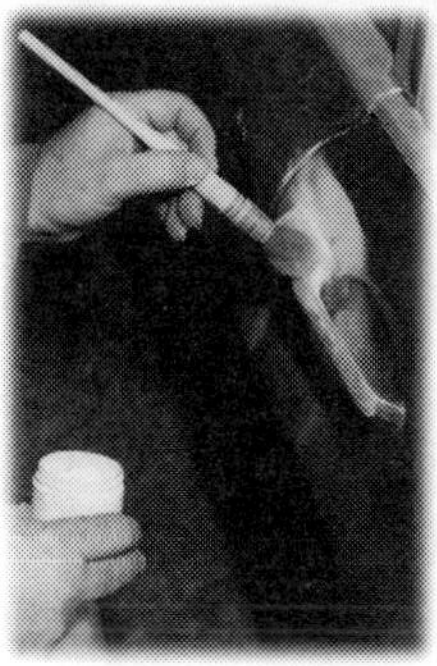

Crime scenes are often dusted for fingerprints.

None of that was any use for tracking down the intruder or intruders who had hurt Mr Kent, of course. Nor was anything in the thick folders of data that Ric had downloaded from the Internet. He had photos of missing children, and details of where they were last seen. He had information about how dogs were trained for different aspects of police work—sniffing out explosives and drugs, finding missing persons and finding bodies. Plenty of information on all sorts of police procedure, but nothing that could help him find the person who attacked Mr Kent. Nothing that could help him decide what to do about Briggsey.

A couple of his books were on self-defence. Before talking to Matt's mother, he thought that you had to learn karate and be a black belt to defend yourself against an attacker. Then he learned that even a set of keys could be used as a weapon.

"Look at this," he said to Matt, holding up the page that showed how someone's body weight could be used against them. "I'd better learn how to do this if I want to get away from Briggsey."

Matt grunted. "I'd just stay as far away from him as you can. Don't get within reach."

"Oh sure," said Ric. "To do that, I'd have to become a hermit."

Then they heard the front door slam. Quick footsteps sounded down the hall, and the door to Gabby's room slammed too. Then something heavy was thrown against the wall between his room and Gabby's.

"Wow," said Matt. "She's mad about something."

"She's always like that," said Ric. Ever

Aikido is a Japanese martial art that uses an opponent's weight to overpower them.

since he could remember, Gabby had had a short temper. He could remember her pinching him and slapping him when he was little. His mother always told her off when she did it, but it didn't seem to make her stop. He'd overheard his mother yelling at Gabby one day, telling her that if she didn't learn to control her temper she'd end up like Uncle Alessandro. The family didn't talk about him much. He was often in trouble with the police. They had often been called to the house by the neighbours when he fought with his wife. Ric didn't like Uncle Alessandro. None of them did. Even his wife had taken out some sort of court order to keep him away from her and her kids.

People who are abused by their partners can go to court and get an order which stops the violent person coming near the victim.

Matt suddenly spoke up. "I've been thinking."

Ric started putting his crime books back on the shelf. "I hope you've got an idea, because I'm fresh out."

"About Briggsey," Matt said thoughtfully. "Okay, he told you not to tell on Gabby for sneaking out to see him—but he seems pretty keen to stop you asking questions about him and his gang, doesn't he? I was wondering…do

A magnifying glass is a symbol of crime detection because it was the first tool used by investigators to help find clues at a crime scene.

you think he knows more than he's letting on about the bashing?"

Ric turned to look at Matt. He'd been so worried about what Briggsey might do to him, that he hadn't thought of that. But Matt was right. Briggsey was trying to stop him asking questions. Was he worried that Ric might stumble across something? "You're right," he said. "Briggsey and Chris Papandreou. I bet they both know."

Then he felt a sudden lurch in his chest. And if those two knew more than they were letting on, then it was more than likely Gabby did too. Last night she had been with Briggsey until just before midnight.

Maybe Briggsey even did it. Mr Kent's grandson said he was bad. Oh no. He felt sick. What was a person supposed to do if they found out one of their own family was involved in something? But Gabby couldn't be. She liked Mr Kent. She wouldn't have been involved in anything that would harm him. Would she?

Matt looked at his watch. "I've got to get home and help Dad pack some boxes

domestic violence: *repeated violent acts among people who live in the same house.*

this afternoon. Do you want to come too? We could phone Mum at the station and tell her about Briggsey and what he said. The police could question them." He grinned. "Hey, we might be the ones with the information to break the case!"

Ric felt a rush of panic. If the police questioned Briggsey about where he'd been the night before, they'd find out Gabby had been with him. They'd come to interview Gabby too. What would his parents say if they realised that Ric was responsible for bringing the police to their home? For getting Gabby into trouble?

"Don't say anything to your mum just yet," he said quickly. "Let me see if I can get anything else out of Gabby, right? Then I'll come over to your house and tell you what I've found out."

"Okay." Matt got up from the floor and handed Ric the last couple of books he'd been flicking through. "I bet I'm right. I bet they know a lot more than they're saying. I wouldn't be surprised if one of them did it. See you soon. Don't be long!" He left the room. A moment later Ric heard the back door open and close.

When a phone or room is "bugged" small devices are hidden to pick-up and transmit all conversations.

It is an offence to record someone's telephone conversation without telling them they are being taped.

Ric was glad he'd gone. He went to the window and looked out, remembering Gabby sneaking out a couple of nights before. The sound of Briggsey's car taking off. And now he'd been warned to stop asking questions....

What was he going to do? He wished he'd never started poking into things. It was okay for Matt; it wasn't his sister who was possibly involved. Ric groaned. He didn't know. He couldn't think. And he had the beginning of a headache.

Then Gabby's door opened. He heard her footsteps moving quickly to the kitchen. A moment later he could hear her talking in a low voice on the phone.

Okay, so you weren't supposed to listen in on other people's conversations. But he decided to do it anyway. Ric moved quietly down the hall, his feet making no sound on the carpet. He stopped just before the door to the kitchen. And what he heard made his blood freeze.

"...he suspects something, I know he does," Gabby was saying. "First he spies on me. Then he asks me to ask you and Chris what you know. Then today we see him coming out of that old bat Conroy's place—right next door! Steve told him to stop asking questions and to keep his mouth shut, but he's been talking to that cop's son. Jeez, if he doesn't stop we're gonna get in big trouble…" She stopped to listen and then said, "Yeah, okay. I'll see you there in about ten minutes."

Gabby not only knew something; she was obviously in it up to her neck. Ric thought about ducking back into his room so she wouldn't know he'd overheard, then felt a surge of anger at the thought of old Mr Kent. Blow it, he was going to ask her. He moved forward into the kitchen, just as Gabby put down the phone. Her head jerked up when she saw him, and her eyes narrowed. He could tell from her face that she knew he'd overheard.

"Sneaking around as usual," she said. She folded her arms and leaned back against the kitchen counter in a tough-guy attitude, just staring him down. "I thought you and your little spy friend had left."

"He did," Ric said. "I didn't. Good thing, too. Now I know—Briggsey's involved in all this, isn't he? And Papandreou. But what about you, Gabby? Were you with them?"

Gabby moved toward him. She leaned forward and hissed in his face, "Mind your own business. Stay away from my friends. And keep your mouth shut." With that, she gave him a two-handed shove that sent him sprawling on the floor and stormed out of the house.

chapter 6

I told them to stop

RIC SAT UP and rubbed the back of his head. He'd cracked it on the breakfast bar on the way down, and it hurt like mad. For a moment he just sat there, feeling hopeless. And scared.

He heaved himself up, and leaned on the breakfast bar. He needed time. First, try to put Matt off for a while. Think about what to do. The same question kept going round in his head: had Gabby been there when Mr Kent was robbed? Or had it happened after she got home?

And if he did find out she'd been there…what then? Were you supposed to tell on members of your own family? It would have been all right if he hadn't set out to find who had robbed Mr Kent. Now he didn't know what to do. There must have been police officers that found

If you know that a serious crime has been committed and you don't tell police about it, then you can be charged for withholding evidence.

out their families had done something wrong. What did they do? Did they have to give evidence in court? Did they make you tell?

If Mr Kent died, the people who did it were going to be charged with murder.

Questions, questions. He needed more time. He'd have to put Matt off…and Matt's mother. Ric thought again of that cold stare she could turn on, and shivered. What if she didn't want Matt to hang out with him any more? What if she thought that he might turn out like Gabby?

He gave Matt another ten minutes to get home, then phoned him. "Hi," he said. "I can't come over this afternoon, right? I've got to help Mum in the shop." He hoped Matt couldn't tell that he was lying. "Gabby's not telling me much." Well, *that* was true. If he hadn't overheard her, he'd know nothing. "I reckon Briggsey probably knows who did the job, though, and he's trying to protect whoever it was. So is Gabby. Don't say anything to your mum yet, okay? I'll see if I can find out more. See you, man." He hung up, and considered his next move. If only there was someone he could talk it over with. But there was nobody. Nobody who wouldn't tell the cops. Or his parents.

What he really wanted to do was to go and hide somewhere. Curl up in a cave for a few months until all this went away.

What if Gabby had to go to a detention centre? Mum and Dad would be sad. Sad, and angry, and embarrassed. What a mess.

In the end, he just sat in his room and visited crime sites on the Internet. If he went outside the house, Briggsey or Papandreou might be waiting for him. Gabby was sure to tell them that he had guessed they were in it. At least he was safe at home.

But then, Mr Kent hadn't been safe in his own home, had he?

Gabby came rushing back home about an hour and a half after she'd left, flinging open the door to his room. She looked pale and on edge.

"Did you say anything to Matt? Or his dumb detective mother?" she demanded.

"No." Ric swung around on his student's chair to look at her, his back to

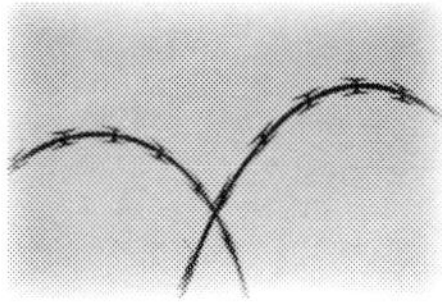

Juvenile detention centres are like prisons but they are for offenders under 18 years of age. Juveniles may be locked in at night and the centre may be surrounded by high security fences.

his computer. "Why? What's happened?"

Gabby looked ill. Her voice was actually trembling. "Briggsey. They've taken him into the police station for questioning. From right outside the shop." She swallowed. "He won't say anything about me being there, I know he won't. So don't you either, right? Don't say a single word about me going out."

Ric's heart seemed to drop about ten centimetres in his chest. "So you were there with them. In Mr Kent's house."

"I didn't hit him," she said, sitting on the edge of Ric's bed. "I didn't touch him, honest. I tried to stop them." She avoided his shocked gaze. "Nobody meant to hurt him. He just rushed up and Briggsey shoved him away. Then one of the others pushed him around a bit...I told them to stop it..."

For a moment Ric couldn't speak. His own sister had been in there stealing stuff from Mr Kent. "You rat," he said. "You rotten, dirty, rat..." He wanted to say more, but the words wouldn't come out.

"I told them to stop," she said. "I like Mr Kent. I didn't want them to hurt him. I just thought they'd take the TV and video and go. He's half deaf...he was supposed to be asleep; I told them he wouldn't hear us."

This was getting worse and worse. Ric wasn't sure if he was hearing right. "You mean you told them to steal his things?"

"He can get new ones," said Gabby impatiently. "They would have been insured. It should have been easy. Everything would have been all right if he hadn't woken up." She grabbed his wrist. "The others won't say anything about me being with Briggsey. Mum and Dad think I was here all night. So you have to say the same."

"No," said Ric.

"You have to." Gabby dug her fingers into his arm, until Ric pulled it away and stood up to get away from her. "I need an alibi. Matt's mother will believe you. And I don't want to go to some kids' home. I don't want to go to court." She stood up, looking at him eye-to-eye. "And Briggsey said he'd bash me as well as you if you said anything. Please, Ric, I won't do anything like this again. Honest!"

Ric didn't even want to look at her. Gabby only ever said "please" when it suited her. It made him angry. He shook his head. "I can't."

Police stations have cells where they keep people who have been arrested before they are taken to gaol.

"Think of Mum and Dad," she said insistently. "Can you imagine if they have to go to the police station? It'll be your fault if they have to. If you just say I was here all night, everything will be okay."

"It's too late." Ric glared at her. "It's too late! Matt knows. I told him you sneaked out. And he saw Briggsey threatening me. So did what's his name, that grandson of Mr Kent…Ray."

"Oh, great!" Gabby folded her arms, then unfolded them again. She kicked his chair so it went spinning across the room. "Just great! My own brother drops me in it." She swore violently and swept the disks and schoolbooks next to the computer off the desk onto the floor.

"Get out of here," said Ric, rushing over to stand in front of the computer. He hated Gabby's temper. Usually he was even a bit scared of it, but today he was so angry he didn't care what he said to her. "Out! OUT!"

With a final slap that made his head ring, Gabby stormed out. A moment later he heard more bangs; more objects hitting the wall in her room. Ric knew this mood. She'd wrecked her room before.

Ric left. He had to get out of here. Just

as he'd expected, things were getting worse and worse.

At least Ric didn't have to worry about being chased by Briggsey if he'd been taken away for questioning. It was safe to walk the streets—for a little while. He walked for almost an hour, all the way to Timezone in the shopping mall, and sat there out of sight of the rest of the world, playing games until it was nearly dark.

The words kept going round in his head: *What am I going to do? What am I going to do?* It was impossible to concentrate on anything. He kept wondering what would happen to him; what would happen to Gabby. Would he be, made to testify in court because he had a record of Gabby's comings and goings? Did you have to testify against your own family? These were all questions Matt's mother could have answered, but he could hardly ask her now. He wished there was someone he could talk to.

Finally he had no money left. He couldn't put it off any longer anyway. He had to go home. Had to find out what was happening. He started walking home again. About half way there, a car tooted then pulled up beside him. It was Matt's dad.

He got out of the car and leaned on the roof. "Hey, Ric," he said. "I've been looking for you. Want a lift?"

Fear crawled up Ric's spine. "Why? What's happened?"

"You're eating at our place tonight. Hop in."

Slowly Ric opened the door and slid into the passenger seat. If he was eating at the Taylor's place, then that meant his mother wasn't at home. But his mother was *always* home to cook dinner. His dad looked after the shop, and his mum came home. Unless there was some kind of emergency.

"Your mum's had to stay at the shop," said Matt's dad. "Your dad was called away."

"Called away where?"

"He's out looking for Gabby, Ric," Mr Taylor said gently. "It looks like she might be able to help the police with some information about the robbery—but they can't find her. They couldn't find you, either."

If children are missing, family and friends often go to known play areas, friends' houses or shopping centres to look for them.

Ric stared at his knees, feeling a big red tide of shame sweep through him. It was all coming out. Everyone would know that his sister had broken into Mr Kent's house. Maybe they were only questioning her because she was a friend of Briggsey's. Maybe they didn't know yet that she had actually been in the house. Even if they took her fingerprints, that wouldn't prove anything. She could have left them there when she delivered groceries, just like he had. Did they even take fingerprints of under-age people? Or wasn't that allowed? He'd have to ask Matt's mum. No…he couldn't ask her; she'd know why he was asking.

"You okay?"

Ric jumped as though Mr Taylor had been able to read his thoughts. "Yes," he muttered, not looking at him. Gosh, here he was trying to think of ways Gabby could get out of it. If it had been anybody but his sister, he would have been telling the police everything he could find out. He couldn't believe he was protecting Gabby. "You don't have to feed me. There's food at home."

"That's okay. We told your mum you

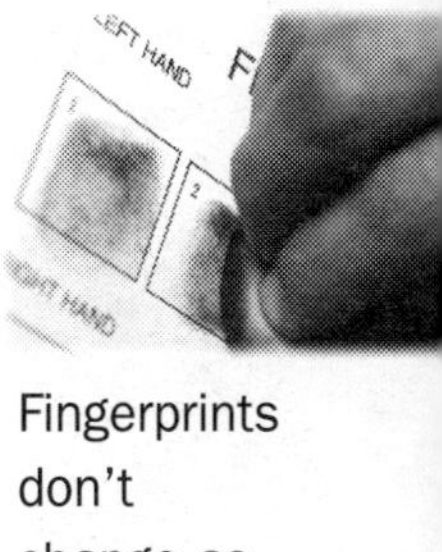

Fingerprints don't change as people age.

Police usually wait 24 hours before listing a person as missing because most missing people contact someone within that time.

could eat at our place. Gives her one less thing to worry about. Your brother's at his friend's place." There was silence for a moment, then "She didn't know where you or Gabby were, and it was getting dark."

"Well, I'm not a baby. Lots of my friends stay out after dark."

"True enough," said Mr Taylor soothingly. "I guess we parents worry because it's so easy to get into trouble without intending to. We just don't want you to get hurt."

Ric thought about Briggsey's threats in broad daylight in the middle of a sunny Saturday. It didn't have to be dark for bad things to happen.

In five minutes, they were at the Taylors' place. Matt came out of the front door as soon as he heard the car. "Hey," he said "Where'd you get to?"

"Timezone," said Ric. How much did Matt know? How much did any of the Taylors know?

"Well, I'll just go cook some dinner, guys," said Matt's dad. "I'll give you a call when it's ready." He disappeared into the kitchen.

"I stayed home in case you phoned," said Matt, "while Dad went looking in the car."

Ric frowned. "Why was everyone looking for me?"

Matt led the way into the TV room at the back of the house. "Mum went to see your dad, and they both went to your place to see Gabby. She wasn't there. You weren't there either, but your room was trashed, man. Yours and Gabby's. Nobody knew what had happened to you."

Ric sat down with a thump. "What do you mean, trashed?"

"Like really trashed. The computer—" Matt shook his head. "Everything. Your books all torn up. The mattress on the floor."

"My books? My crime books?" Ric couldn't believe it.

Matt shrugged. "I didn't see it, it was only what your dad said. And with Briggsey after you, they didn't know if you were in real trouble. Or Gabby." He looked embarrassed. "I had to tell them. About Briggsey threatening you. I didn't know if he'd got to you. But then Mum said he was already at the police station."

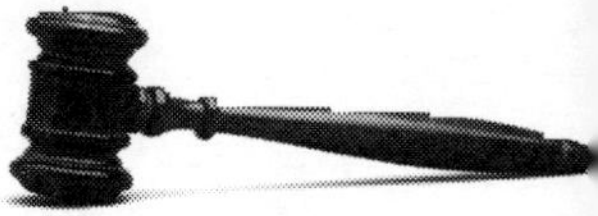

Gavels are wooden hammers or mallets. They have traditionally been used by judges to keep order in the courtroom. The judge will bang with the gavel to gain the court's attention.

People who plan a crime can be prosecuted even if they get someone else to actually carry it out.

Ric sighed. It was all coming out. He couldn't keep it to himself any more.

"Gabby was there, Matt," he said. "At Mr Kent's place. She told me this afternoon. She said she tried to stop them hurting him, but—" He swallowed. "It was because of her they broke in. She told them he'd be asleep. That it would be easy to take his stuff." He looked up at Matt, who was standing open-mouthed looking at him. "She wanted me to say that she'd been in all night. Give her an alibi. I said no."

"So who trashed your room?" Matt frowned. "If Briggsey is at the police station…was it Chris Papandreou?"

Ric gave a sour laugh. "Papandreou? No. No, it was Gabby, you can bet on it. You heard her throwing things today—she's got a rotten temper. I heard her chucking more stuff around in her room before I left. Looks like she started on mine next, then left before Mum and Dad came home."

"Wow." Matt's eyes were huge. "So d'you think she's run away?"

"I wouldn't be surprised," said Ric moodily. "She's done it before. But this is the first time she's had the police after her."

chapter 7
The search

NOBODY could find Gabby that night. Or the next. The police were circulating her description. They were questioning all her friends. But nobody knew where she was. Or if they did, they weren't saying.

Now Ric knew exactly what happened when someone went missing. Usually the police waited twenty-four hours before listing someone as missing—unless it was a child at risk—but with Gabby, it was different. She was wanted by police for her involvement in the robbery. Despite Gabby's certainty that Steven Briggs wouldn't tell the police that she was with him, he had told them everything. Including the fact that it was all her idea. She had apparently told the gang that Mr Kent was old and couldn't move about very well because of his bad leg, that he was a bit deaf in one ear and that he went to bed early. She knew where he kept the spare key too, because she had seen him get it from under the pot plant one day when she carried some groceries home for him. Gabby was in big trouble.

Ric was horrified when he saw his room. The computer monitor was lying on the floor next to the wall, with the side casing all cracked. There was a big hole where it had hit the wall. His mattress was on the floor, and his crime books were all over the floor, lots of them with pages torn out. She'd taken his surveillance log. His clothes were tipped onto the floor, and drawers lay haphazardly on the bed and on the floor.

Her own room wasn't as bad as his. It was a mess, where she'd thrown things around in a fit of temper, but no worse than other times when she'd lost it. Some of her clothes were missing.

The police came and searched Gabby's room. Ric's mother stayed in the kitchen dabbing at her eyes, while his father watched, grim-faced.

Matt's mother sat Ric down and asked him to tell them what he knew. "I know

A juvenile must have a responsible adult present when being interviewed by the police.

she's your sister, Ric," she said gently. Not a trace of her hard cop's stare. "I know you feel like you're getting her into more trouble. But we already know that she was there when Mr Kent was robbed. It seems that Gabby tried to stop Steven Briggs and John Budiansky when they started using physical violence against Mr Kent, so at least that's something in her favour. We're just filling in the rest of the picture."

Ric's father was sitting there too. "Tell them whatever they want to know, Ricardo," he said, looking old and tired. "If Gabriella has done wrong, she has to suffer the consequences. And..." His voice trembled. "We want to try to find her. Anything you can tell the police might help."

It seemed it didn't matter what he said now anyway—they already knew what had happened. It seemed that they had been keeping an eye on Briggsey and his friends for some time, suspecting that they were involved in a series of break-and-enters around the area. And when they got a search warrant for Briggsey's

search warrant: *authority to search premises.*

place, they found a stash of stolen goods—including the little CD player from Mr Kent's kitchen.

Ric thought he'd better tell Detective Taylor about Gabby sneaking out at night. He couldn't look at his father when he described his surveillance log and the way he saw Gabby getting into Briggsey's car one night. He showed them the book with the torn-out pages.

Matt's mother wasn't quick enough to hide a glint of disapproval. Ric swallowed hard. "You don't think I should have kept track of Gabby like that? Do you?"

"Well, no. People deserve to have privacy, Ric, whether they're doing the wrong thing or not. How would you have felt if you knew that your little brother Tony was watching everything you did?" She smiled to take the sting out of her words. "I know you're keen to learn everything you can about law enforcement and detection, Ric, but you do have to be careful not to trample all over people's rights. The police can't just follow people around and spy on them, or obtain information whenever they feel like it. If we don't have a good reason for

A search warrant for a particular location can be issued by a magistrate if the police have reason to believe that they will find evidence about a crime at that location.

looking up information about people, we can be charged. Even lose our jobs."

Ric hung his head a bit lower, and hastily moved on to the next thing. Gabby hadn't found his book with the observation details in it, because it had been in his school bag. A bit nervously, he handed that over, with all the details about Gabby's rings and the devil tattoo below her shoulder blade. He heard his father gasp when he told Matt's mother about that. He muttered "Ah, Gabriella!" in a broken voice.

Matt's mother turned the pages with interest, reading his descriptions of people. "So Briggsey has a chipped tooth, does he? You've done a good job recording this, Ric," she said. She smiled at him. "You will make a good detective one day, you know."

> Officers need a password to log on to the police database and a record is kept of their use of the system.

Ric shrugged. He still felt all tight inside with everything that had happened. Did he still want to be a detective, trying to talk to people who threatened you and refused to talk to you? Did he want to deal with people like Gabby and Briggsey all the time?

Matt's mother seemed to read his mind. "I know all this is hard on you and your family, Ric," she said. "But it makes you a better police officer if you know what it's like to be a victim. If you know what it's like for families caught up in things like this. And the information you've given us about Gabby's tattoo and her rings might help us to find her."

"What will happen to her?" Ric asked. "Will she go to court? Will she have charges laid? And have to go to a detention centre?"

"If we find her, yes, she'll have to appear in a children's court. She's fourteen, so she'll be treated as a minor. Luckily Mr Kent is on the mend now, so she and the rest of them aren't facing murder charges. But she'll be charged with break, enter and steal, assault and rob, and grievous bodily harm. Mr Kent has a few broken ribs, and they weren't caused by his fall.

She hesitated. "Unfortunately, Gabby's already had a couple of cautions for shoplifting and assault on another girl. That's not going to look good. If she is found guilty her sentence could be anything from twelve months to two years."

Shoplifting? Assault? Ric was stunned.

Sometimes judges and magistrates take into account circumstances which might excuse the criminal behaviour. They then hand down a lesser sentence.

He didn't know about that. He looked at his father, who nodded sadly. "Yes, Ricardo, we have had to appear at the police station for Gabriella before. We tried to keep it from you and Antonio."

In a way, Ric hoped they didn't find Gabby. It would be a lot more peaceful around home with her gone. Then he looked at his father sitting there with his shoulders slumped. His mum and dad would always worry if they didn't find her. Even after she'd caused them so much trouble.

A few weeks later, when Mr Kent had been home from hospital for a while, Ric took him a big bag of groceries. He didn't know whether Mr Kent would want to see him or not. Maybe he didn't trust the Morelli family any more.

Police usually record all interviews. Suspects receive a copy of the tape.

But Mr Kent was just as nice as ever. He opened a packet of biscuits. "Look, young Ric," he said, "there's often a bad apple in the barrel. That happens in lots of families. Some of them straighten up later on, some of them don't." He gave Daisy a biscuit. Even though his home had been broken into, he didn't want a big dog. He was happy with Daisy, even though she couldn't defend him against a fly. He had put new locks on the doors though. "Just look at my grandson Ray. Now there's one who was in lots of trouble when he was a youngster. I know he still looks a bit rough, but he's a lot better now—he's got a good job as a mechanic and he hasn't been in trouble for ages." He laughed. "Your Gabby might turn out all right in the end. Or she might not. But it's not your fault."

That made Ric feel a lot better. He knew it would make his mum and dad feel better too. They had offered Mr Kent groceries any time he wanted them, as they were so ashamed of what Gabby had done.

When they found out that Mr Kent hadn't been insured after all, they had bought him a new TV and video too, because the ones Briggsey and his gang stole didn't turn up. Matt's mother went around to see how he was too. She and Mr Kent seemed to get on pretty well.

"She's a nice woman, that Detective Taylor," Mr Kent told Ric. "They tell me you want to be a detective too. Interested in crime scenes." He grinned.

In Missing Person's Week people who have lost contact with their families are encouraged to phone home, free of charge, to reassure their relatives.

Prison inmates are given only the basic necessities. Loss of the ordinary comforts that we may take for granted is part of their punishment.

"I don't know," said Ric, blushing. So Mrs Conroy had told him about Ric wanting to see the crime scene. How embarrassing. "I did want to. Now I'm not sure."

"Well, you think about it," said Mr Kent. "Sounds to me like you'd be a good person to be looking out for people like me." He bent down and patted Daisy. "Specially when our dogs aren't too good at it, eh Daisy?"

Two months went by, and Gabby still hadn't come home or been in contact. They all thought she might have gone to one of the big cities.

"Gabby might come home again one day, Ric," Detective Taylor told him. "In six months, a year—when she feels that everything has died down a bit. Or she might stay away for years. Some people never come home again. But your description will help. She can change the colour and length of her hair, but that devil tattoo will identify her. She might phone in Missing Person's Week next

statute of limitations: *the time after which a person can no longer be charged.*

month just to let you all know that she's all right."

"What about if she does come home?" he asked. "Will she still have to go to court? Even if it's a year? Two years?"

"I'm afraid so, Ric. She's wanted for involvement in a crime. She'll have to answer to that, even if she leaves it for twenty years." Matt's mother shrugged. "There's no statute of limitations on this crime. She'll have to come home and take the consequences. Maybe she'll learn from her mistakes."

As Briggsey hadn't learnt. Three weeks after the robbery, Steven Briggs and his friends had to appear in court. Their charges were the same as Gabby's would be: break, enter and steal; assault and rob; assault occasioning grievous bodily harm and handling stolen goods—not just Mr Kent's, but other people's property as well.

A prima facie case was established, and six months later, after a trial by jury, Briggsey was sent to prison for five years.

If someone commits a crime as a juvenile they are charged in a children's court even if they are over 18 when finally arrested.

prima facie: *latin for "at first sight" it means there is enough evidence to go to trial.*

That made Ric feel relieved. At least he was safe from him for a while. More than anything else, it was the satisfaction of helping to put Briggsey away that made Ric decide that he did, after all, want to go ahead with his plans to be a detective.

After a while, he started building up his collection of crime books again. When he discussed it with Matt's mother, he felt that sense of excitement again…yes, this was what he wanted to do!

But, he decided, there was one thing he wasn't going to do again—keep a surveillance log on his family. It wasn't only Detective Taylor who thought he'd gone too far with that. His mum and dad were annoyed too.

"No more practising on your family, Ricardo," his father said firmly. "No spying! No making notes!" Then he slapped Ric on the back. "But maybe your seeing Gabriella's tattoo will help us find her one day. And if she hasn't come back when you are a detective, maybe you can help to find her. Yes?"

"Sure, Dad," said Ric. "I'll do that." Secretly, he didn't expect to find Gabby unless she wanted to be found. But meeting up with Gabby again was just a small part of his future. What felt good now was that he felt sure he knew what he really wanted—a career in detection.

Where to from here?

Interested in finding out more about crime and detection? If you visit your local library you may be lucky enough to find a librarian like Di Eagleton, who helped me find information for this book. Librarians can not only put you in touch with books and articles but help you to find Internet sites as well.

If you have access to the Internet at home, type "police procedure" or "forensic science" into the search engine.

The Internet address: http://www.children-missing.org has information about missing children.

Other sites are: http://www.cops.aust.com; http://www.studyweb.com; and to find books on crime and detection, http://www.amazon.com.

If you're interested in mystery stories, there are many great books such as the adventures of Nancy Drew and the Hardy Boys. You might also like to read *Letters from the Inside* by John Marsden,

45 & 47 Stella Street and *Everything that Happened* by Elizabeth Honey.

A good place to start finding out more is the companion volume in the Phenomena series *Crime in Time,* which will give the facts on crime.

Happy hunting! Maybe you'll be interested enough to want to become a detective yourself one day.

Marg's note

I like reading mysteries. I like reading about how police investigate a case, and gradually put together information to find out who is guilty. My interest in police procedure and in how police prevent crime, led to my spending twelve months as a Volunteer in Policing (a civilian who spends some time each week assisting in police duties). That's where I picked up a lot of the information for this book. Senior Constable Peter Gavin of the NSW Police Service also checked the story for accuracy. Police have to get the facts right if they want to prosecute a crime, so I wanted to make sure my facts were right in Ric's story, too!

I have spent time on Community Aid Panels for juvenile offenders, so I have seen children like the ones in this story. Not everybody who breaks the law goes on to a life of crime. Many young people get cautioned and never re-offend.

I believe we can all do a bit to help combat crime, by looking out for each other and becoming "crime conscious". If the community and police work together, our neighbourhoods can become safer and happier places.

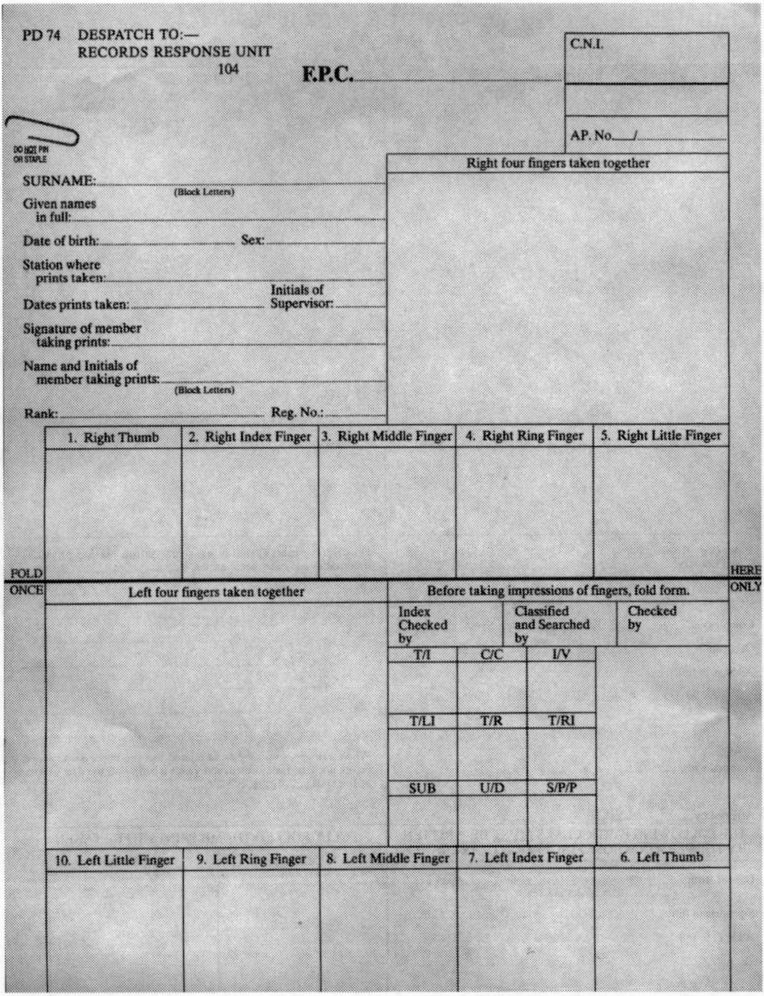

PD 74 DESPATCH TO:—
RECORDS RESPONSE UNIT
104

F.P.C. ....

C.N.I.
AP. No. ___/

DO NOT PIN OR STAPLE

SURNAME: .... (Block Letters)

Given names in full: ....

Date of birth: .... Sex: ....

Station where prints taken: ....

Dates prints taken: .... Initials of Supervisor: ....

Signature of member taking prints: ....

Name and Initials of member taking prints: .... (Block Letters)

Rank: .... Reg. No.: ....

Right four fingers taken together

1. Right Thumb	2. Right Index Finger	3. Right Middle Finger	4. Right Ring Finger	5. Right Little Finger

FOLD ONCE HERE ONLY

Left four fingers taken together

Before taking impressions of fingers, fold form.

Index Checked by	Classified and Searched by	Checked by

T/I	C/C	I/V
T/LI	**T/R**	**T/RI**
SUB	**U/D**	**S/P/P**

10. Left Little Finger	9. Left Ring Finger	8. Left Middle Finger	7. Left Index Finger	6. Left Thumb

A police fingerprint record.

RIGHT Palm	LEFT Palm

Birthplace—Town and Country: ....

Height: .... Build: .... Racial Appearance: ....

Complexion: .... Hair: .... Eyes: ....

Occupation: ....

Address in full: ....

Offence: ....

Arrested with: ....

Arrested by: ....

Descriptive marks, including scars, tattoo marks, physical deformities and other peculiarities, etc.: ....

When a finger is missing or so injured that the impression cannot be obtained, or is deformed, and yields a bad print, the date of loss of finger or injury **must** be stated.

THE FOLLOWING PARTICULARS **MUST** BE WRITTEN BY THE PERSON WHOSE FINGERPRINTS ARE TAKEN

Date of Birth: .... Age: ....
(Day Month and Year)

Signature in full: ....

Address in full: ....

FULLY ROLLED THUMB PRINTS TO BE TAKEN

Right Thumb	Left Thumb